A NOTE TO PARENTS

When your children are ready to "step into reading," giving them the right books—and lots of them—is as crucial as giving them the right food to eat. **Step into Reading Books** present exciting stories and information reinforced with lively, colorful illustrations that make learning to read fun, satisfying, and worthwhile. They are priced so that acquiring an entire library of them is affordable. And they are beginning readers with an important difference—they're written on four levels.

Step 1 Books, with their very large type and extremely simple vocabulary, have been created for the very youngest readers. **Step 2 Books** are both longer and slightly more difficult. **Step 3 Books,** written to mid-second-grade reading levels, are for the child who has acquired even greater reading skills. **Step 4 Books** offer exciting nonfiction for the increasingly proficient reader.

Children develop at different ages. **Step into Reading Books,** with their four levels of reading, are designed to help children become good—and interested—readers *faster.* The grade levels assigned to the four steps—preschool through grade 1 for Step 1, grades 1 through 3 for Step 2, grades 2 and 3 for Step 3, and grades 2 through 4 for Step 4—are intended only as guides. Some children move through all four steps very rapidly; others climb the steps over a period of several years. These books will help your child "step into reading" in style!

The author and the illustrator wish to thank
the experts who supplied information to help
make our text and pictures historically
accurate. We are especially grateful to the
research staff at Plimoth Plantation.

Text copyright © 1990 by Linda Hayward. Illustrations copyright © 1990 by James Watling. All
rights reserved under International and Pan-American Copyright Conventions. Published in the
United States by Random House, Inc., New York, and simultaneously in Canada by Random House of
Canada Limited, Toronto.

Library of Congress Cataloging-in-Publication Data:
Hayward, Linda. The first Thanksgiving. (Step into reading. A Step 2 book) Summary: Describes how
the first Thanksgiving celebration came to be. 1. Thanksgiving Day–Juvenile literature.   2. Pilgrims
(New Plymouth Colony)–Juvenile literature.   3. Massachusetts–History–New Plymouth, 1620–1691
–Juvenile literature. [1. Thanksgiving Day.   2. Pilgrims (New Plymouth Colony)   3. Massachusetts–
History–New Plymouth, 1620–1691]   I. Watling, James, ill.   II. Title.   III. Series: Step into read-
ing. Step 2 book. F68.H295 1990   394.2′683   90-52517
ISBN 0-679-80218-5 (pbk.) ISBN 0-679-90218-X (lib. bdg.)

Manufactured in the United States of America
20 19 18 17 16

STEP INTO READING is a trademark of Random House, Inc.

Step into Reading

THE FIRST THANKSGIVING

By Linda Hayward
Illustrated by James Watling

A Step 2 Book

Random House New York

Plymouth, England—1620.

A ship is in the harbor

taking on passengers.

The people going aboard

seem too poor

and too ordinary

to ever be famous.

And yet their names

are now in history books.

Now, almost 400 years later,

we still tell their story.

These are the people
we call the Pilgrims.
They are about to sail
to a strange new land
called America.
They've been warned that
Indians may attack them.
Even the voyage
will be dangerous.

There may be
pirates or hurricanes.
Many a ship has sailed off
and never been seen again.
The Pilgrims are risking
their lives.
Why?

It started with the king.

The king declared that everybody

must belong to his religion.

The Pilgrims wanted

their own religion.

They tried meeting in secret.

But the king sent spies to watch
their houses.
He sent soldiers to arrest
their leaders.
Even their neighbors
turned against them.
So the Pilgrims decided
to leave England.

Now at last they are on the ship

that will take them across the ocean—

the *Mayflower.*

Other people have joined them.

Everyone hopes for a better life

in America.

They have given up their houses.

They have said good-bye
to their friends.

They have said good-bye
to England, too.

The *Mayflower* is on its way.

The ship is crowded—

there are 102 passengers in all!

Most of them must stay

in one stuffy place below the deck.

It is cold and damp.

There is no water for washing,

no toilet.

Every day the Pilgrims eat
the same meal—pickled beef,
cheese, and dry, hard bread.
Some of the bread
is full of worms.
Even the water tastes bad.

Halfway across the ocean

the *Mayflower* is hit

by terrible storms.

Week after week

huge waves crash

across the deck.

It seems as if

the small ship

will break in two.

But the *Mayflower* is still afloat

after nine long weeks at sea.

One morning a lookout spots

a dark speck ahead.

Land!

What a thrilling sight!

They have reached their new home.

The ship gets closer.

The Pilgrims see a sandy beach

and many trees.

America looks wild and strange.

Is it safe?

Are Indians hiding in the forest?

A search party goes ashore.

The men walk along

for miles and miles.

Suddenly they see Indians!

But the Indians are frightened

and run away.

The men keep exploring.

They find wonderful things—

corn, baskets, a spring.

They take fresh water

back to the ship.

How sweet it tastes!

Now the Pilgrims must choose

a good place to live—

a place with a harbor, and fresh water,

and fields for planting.

At last they find the perfect spot.

Here a brook
flows into the harbor.
A big rock marks the landing.
They will call this place
New Plymouth.

The Pilgrims begin a new life

in a new land.

There is so much to do.

They must build houses

before they can leave the ship.

But it is winter.

Bad weather slows them down.

It takes weeks

to finish just one house.

And there is hardly enough to eat.

The Pilgrims survive

on food from the ship, roots,

wild birds, and shellfish.

How they wish for

a dish of pudding

and a slice of beef!

On a nearby hill
the Pilgrims make a platform
for their cannons.
They know the Indians
are watching them.
They can see smoke
from their campfires.
They can hear them
in the woods.
A guard is posted
day and night.

How hard that first winter is!

Every day is bleak and cold.

Fierce, icy winds rip through

the settlement.

Freezing rain falls for hours.

The Pilgrims huddle together

by their fires.

They feel miserable and so alone!

Almost everyone gets sick.

Many people die.

The small Pilgrim band

gets smaller and smaller.

By the end of winter

only half of the Pilgrims

are still alive.

The Pilgrims bury the dead
at night in secret graves.
The Indians must not know
how few Pilgrims are left.
And how weak those few are!

The long sad winter passes,

and spring arrives.

Indians are sighted nearby.

They come closer and closer.

Then one day an Indian

walks right into the settlement.

The children are terrified.

But the Indian smiles and says,

"Welcome."

His name is Samoset.

He speaks English!

He learned it from sea captains.

The Pilgrims ask Samoset

many questions.

They give him presents.

They want to trust

this friendly Indian.

Samoset comes back

with an Indian named Squanto.

Squanto speaks even better English!

He likes the Pilgrims

and he decides to live with them.

He shows them how to survive

in the wilderness—how to hunt for deer,

and where to find berries and herbs.

He also shows them how
to plant corn the Indian way.
The Indians put fish in the ground
when they plant their seed.
The fish make the soil richer.

The Pilgrims want to make friends
with all their Indian neighbors.
Squanto and Samoset tell them
about an Indian king
called Massasoit (mass-uh-SO-it).
He is a great and wise leader.
Massasoit comes to visit Plymouth.

The Pilgrim governor bows
and kisses the Indian king's hand.
Massasoit bows and kisses
the governor's hand.
Then they talk together.

A treaty is made.

The Pilgrims and the Indians

will not harm each other.

There will be peace.

The Indian leader draws his sign.

The governor writes his name.

This treaty is kept for 54 years!

In April the *Mayflower*

sails back to England.

The Pilgrims are sad to see it leave.

But not one of them leaves with it.

They all want to stay in America.

The Pilgrims work hard all summer.
In the fall the fields are full
of good things to eat.
It is a time of plenty
for the Pilgrims.
How thankful they are!
They have food,
and shelter,
and new friends,
the Indians.

The Pilgrims decide
to invite the Indians
to a thanksgiving feast.
Massasoit promises
to come.

What a surprise!

Massasoit arrives

with ninety Indians!

The Pilgrims are worried.

How can they feed so many people?

But Massasoit knows what to do.

He sends some men into the forest.

They come back with five deer.

Now there is enough

for everyone.

The oldest Pilgrim says
a prayer of thanks.
Then the feast begins.
Everyone eats so much—
turkey, lobster,
goose, deer meat,
onions, pumpkin,
corn bread, berries.

The feast lasts for three days.

People eat and sleep,

then eat again.

The Indians do special dances.

The Pilgrim men run races.

They have shooting matches.

The children play games

like tag and blindman's bluff.

Everyone has a wonderful time.

As the years go by,
more people from England
come to America.
The little town of Plymouth
gets bigger and bigger.
The children of the Pilgrims grow up
and have children of their own.
And they have harvest feasts too.

In 1863 Abraham Lincoln,
the president of
the United States of America,
makes Thanksgiving Day
a national holiday.
The first Thanksgiving
is never forgotten.